LE CORDON BLEU

HOME COLLECTION

·MUFFINS·

PERIPLUS
EDITIONS

contents

recipe ratings ❀ *easy* ❀❀ *a little more care needed* ❀❀❀ *more care needed*

Apple muffins

Moist and sweet, enhanced with the flavor of spices, these muffins are good enough to eat at any time of day, whether breakfast, brunch or afternoon tea.

Preparation time **25 minutes**
Total cooking time **30 minutes**
Makes 6 jumbo muffins

1³/4 **cups self-rising flour**
1¹/4 **cups all-purpose flour**
1¹/2 **teaspoons baking powder**
2 teaspoons ground cinnamon
1 teaspoon ground nutmeg
¹/4 **cup sugar**
²/3 **cup unsalted butter**
¹/4 **cup honey**
2 eggs
²/3 **cup milk**
3 green apples, peeled and
  cut into small chunks
1 teaspoon ground cinnamon, extra
2¹/2 **tablespoons sugar, extra**

1 Preheat the oven to 400°F. Grease a 6-cup jumbo muffin pan with melted butter or oil. Sift the flours, baking powder, cinnamon, nutmeg and sugar into a large bowl, and make a well in the center.

2 Melt the butter and honey in a small saucepan over low heat, stirring constantly until smooth. Remove from the heat. Whisk the eggs and milk together.

3 Add the butter mixture, egg mixture and apple chunks to the well in the dry ingredients all at once. Using a metal spoon, stir until just combined. Do not overmix—the mixture should be lumpy.

4 Spoon the mixture into the muffin pan, filling each cup about three-quarters full. Sprinkle with the combined extra cinnamon and sugar. Bake for 20–25 minutes, or until a skewer comes out clean when inserted into the center of a muffin. Cool the muffins in the pan for 10 minutes before lifting out onto a wire rack. These muffins are delicious sliced in half and served with butter.

Lemon muffins

The soft cream cheese frosting generously spread onto these tangy lemon muffins makes them irresistible. When using lemon rind as a flavoring, it is essential to grate only the yellow skin of the lemon and not the white pith, which will be bitter.

*Preparation time **20 minutes***
*Total cooking time **12 minutes***
Makes 8 standard muffins

2¹/₂ cups self-rising flour
¹/₄ teaspoon baking powder
¹/₂ cup sugar
2 tablespoons grated lemon rind
³/₄ cup buttermilk
1 teaspoon vanilla extract
2 eggs, lightly beaten
¹/₂ cup unsalted butter, melted

FROSTING
1 tablespoon unsalted butter, softened
¹/₂ cup cream cheese
2–3 tablespoons confectioners' sugar
1 tablespoon lemon juice

shreds of lemon rind, to decorate

1 Preheat the oven to 400°F. Grease 8 cups of a 12-cup standard muffin pan with a little melted butter or oil and fill the remaining 4 cups with water. Sift the flour, baking powder and sugar into a large mixing bowl, stir in the lemon rind and make a well in the center.

2 Whisk the buttermilk, vanilla and eggs together.

3 Add the egg mixture and the melted butter to the well in the dry ingredients. Using a metal spoon, stir until the mixture is just combined. Do not overmix—the mixture should be lumpy.

4 Spoon the mixture into 8 cups of the muffin pan, filling each cup about three-quarters full. Bake for 10–12 minutes, or until a skewer comes out clean when inserted into the center of a muffin. Cool in the pan for 5 minutes before lifting out onto a wire rack.

5 To make the frosting, beat the butter and cream cheese with an electric mixer until smooth. Add the confectioners' sugar and lemon juice, and beat until thick and creamy. Spread the frosting over the muffins when they are completely cold. Decorate the top of the frosting with shreds of lemon rind for a tangy flavor.

Banana and ginger muffins

*A subtle combination of banana and ginger, enhanced with the golden
nectar of honey, giving a lovely rich muffin.*

Preparation time **20 minutes**
Total cooking time **25 minutes**
Makes 12 standard muffins

2¹/2 cups self-rising flour
1 teaspoon ground ginger
¹/2 cup firmly packed brown sugar
¹/3 cup finely chopped preserved
   or crystallized ginger (see Chef's tip)
¹/4 cup unsalted butter
3 tablespoons honey
¹/2 cup milk
2 eggs
2 ripe bananas, mashed

TOPPING
¹/2 cup cream cheese, softened
3 tablespoons confectioners' sugar
2 teaspoons finely grated lemon rind

preserved or crystallized ginger, to decorate

1 Preheat the oven to 425°F. Brush a 12-cup standard
muffin pan with melted butter or oil. Sift the flour and
ground ginger together into a large mixing bowl. Stir in
the brown sugar and chopped ginger, and make a well in
the center of the mixture.

2 Place the butter and honey in a small saucepan and
stir over low heat until melted. Remove from the heat.
Whisk the milk and eggs together.

3 Add the butter mixture, egg mixture and the bananas
to the well in the dry ingredients. Stir with a metal
spoon until just combined. Do not overmix—the
mixture should be lumpy. Spoon the mixture into
the muffin pan, filling each cup about three-quarters
full. Bake for 20 minutes, or until a skewer comes
out clean when inserted into the center of a muffin.
Cool the muffins in the pan for 5 minutes, then lift out
onto a wire rack to cool completely before spreading
with the topping.

4 To make the topping, beat the cream cheese,
confectioners' sugar and grated lemon rind until light
and creamy. Spread onto the muffins and decorate with
thin slices of preserved or crystallized ginger.

Chef's tip Whether you use preserved or crystallized
ginger, it's best to rinse the pieces briefly in cool water
to remove the syrup or sugar coating before chopping
or slicing.

Blueberry muffins

These classic muffins may be made with either fresh or frozen blueberries, and are particularly good served warm for breakfast or brunch. Try substituting raspberries or blackberries or a combination of these, gently folding them in to keep them whole.

*Preparation time **15 minutes***
*Total cooking time **30 minutes***
Makes 6 jumbo muffins

3 cups self-rising flour
2/3 cup all-purpose flour
1/2 cup firmly packed brown sugar
1 cup fresh or frozen blueberries
  (see Chef's tip)
2 eggs
1 cup milk
1 teaspoon vanilla extract
1/2 cup unsalted butter, melted
confectioners' sugar, to dust

1 Preheat the oven to 425°F. Brush a 6-cup jumbo muffin pan with melted butter or oil. Sift the flours into a large mixing bowl, stir in the sugar and blueberries, and make a well in the center.

2 Whisk the eggs, milk and vanilla together, and add to the well in the dry ingredients. Add the butter, and stir with a metal spoon until just combined. Do not overmix—the mixture should be lumpy.

3 Spoon the mixture into the muffin pan, filling each cup about three-quarters full. Bake for 30 minutes, or until a skewer comes out clean when inserted into the center of a muffin. Cool the muffins in the pan for 5 minutes before lifting out onto a wire rack. Dust the muffins generously with sifted confectioners' sugar before serving. These muffins are delicious sliced in half and spread with butter.

Chef's tip If using frozen blueberries, use them straight from the freezer. Do not allow them to thaw, or they will discolor the muffin mixture.

White chocolate muffins

*The crunchy topping of sliced almonds provides
a pleasant contrast to the soft white chocolate
and lemon muffin.*

Preparation time **20 minutes**
Total cooking time **25 minutes**
Makes 6 jumbo muffins

3 cups self-rising flour
¹/₂ cup sugar
1¹/₃ cups chopped white chocolate
2 eggs
1¹/₂ cups milk
2 teaspoons finely grated lemon rind
²/₃ cup unsalted butter, melted
¹/₂ cup sliced almonds

1 Preheat the oven to 425°F. Brush a 6-cup jumbo
muffin pan with melted butter or oil. Sift the flour into
a large mixing bowl, stir in the sugar and chocolate, and
make a well in the center.

2 Whisk the eggs, milk and lemon rind together, and
pour into the well in the dry ingredients. Add the
butter, and stir with a metal spoon until the mixture
is just combined. Do not overmix—the mixture should
be lumpy.

3 Spoon the mixture into the muffin pan, filling each
cup to about three-quarters full. Sprinkle sliced
almonds on top of the mixture and gently press them
on. Bake for 25 minutes, or until a skewer comes out
clean when inserted into the center of a muffin. Cool
the muffins in the pan for 5 minutes before lifting out
onto a wire rack.

Raisin muffins

Serve these spicy raisin muffins warm with lightly sweetened whipped butter
as an alternative to plain butter. Try using dried apricots or dates as a substitute for raisins.

*Preparation time **25 minutes***
*Total cooking time **20 minutes***
Makes 12 standard muffins

1¼ cups self-rising flour
I cup whole wheat flour
I¹/2 teaspoons baking powder
¹/2 teaspoon ground ginger
¹/2 teaspoon ground cinnamon
¹/2 cup firmly packed brown sugar
I¹/4 cups raisins
2 eggs
³/4 cup milk
¹/2 cup unsalted butter, melted
confectioners' sugar, to dust

WHIPPED BUTTER
¹/4 cup unsalted butter, softened
¹/4 teaspoon vanilla extract
I tablespoon confectioners' sugar

1 Preheat the oven to 425°F. Brush a 12-cup standard muffin pan with melted butter or oil. Sift the flours, baking powder, ginger and cinnamon into a large mixing bowl, returning the husks from the sifter to the bowl. Stir in the sugar and raisins, and make a well in the center.

2 Whisk the eggs and milk together and add to the well in the dry ingredients along with the melted butter. Using a metal spoon, stir until just combined. Do not overmix—the mixture should be lumpy.

3 Spoon the mixture into the muffin pan, filling each cup about three-quarters full. Bake for 20 minutes, or until a skewer comes out clean when inserted into the center of a muffin. Cool the muffins in the pan for 5 minutes before lifting out onto a wire rack.

4 To make the whipped butter, beat the butter with a wooden spoon in a small bowl until it is light and creamy. Beat in the vanilla and the sifted confectioners' sugar. Dust the muffins with some extra sifted confectioners' sugar before serving with the whipped butter.

English muffins

English muffins were originally lightly split around the edges using a fork, then toasted on both sides, pulled open and spread thickly with butter.

*Preparation time **30 minutes***
  *+ **1 hour 20 minutes** proofing*
*Total cooking time **15 minutes***
Makes 12 muffins

2 teaspoons dried yeast
3 1/3 cups bread or all-purpose flour
1 1/2 teaspoons salt
1 teaspoon sugar
1 teaspoon softened unsalted butter

1 Gently heat 1 cup water in a small saucepan until it feels warm, not hot, to the touch. Remove from the heat and stir in the yeast until it is dissolved.
2 Sift the flour, salt and sugar into a large bowl, make a well in the center and pour in the yeast mixture. Melt the butter (again, it should not be too hot) and pour it into the well. Using your hand with fingers slightly spread apart, gradually bring the flour into the liquid and blend well. Turn the dough out onto a floured work surface and knead for 2–3 minutes, or until smooth.

3 Place the dough in a clean bowl that has been sprinkled with a little flour. Cover with plastic wrap and let stand in a warm place for about 1 hour, or until doubled in size.
4 Sprinkle a baking sheet with flour. Preheat the oven to 425°F. Turn the dough out onto a lightly floured work surface and knead until smooth. Roll the dough to about 1/2 inch thick and, using a 2 3/4-inch plain round cutter dipped in flour, cut out rounds and place them on the baking sheet. Re-roll any leftover dough and repeat. Cover the baking sheet with plastic wrap and let stand in a warm place for 15–20 minutes, or until the muffins have risen slightly. Bake for 15 minutes, turning halfway through the cooking time. Remove from the baking sheet and cool on a wire rack.

Chef's tips These muffins can also be cooked on top of the stove using a griddle or dry heavy-bottomed skillet over low heat. Turn over when each side is lightly browned and cooked through.

English muffins are halved before toasting. They are delicious spread with butter and jam.

Pear and pecan muffins

*The soft cooked pear contributes to the lovely moist texture of these muffins
with the added crunch and flavor of chopped toasted pecans.*

Preparation time **25 minutes**
Total cooking time **30 minutes**
Makes 6 jumbo muffins

2 1/2 cups self-rising flour
1 1/4 cups all-purpose flour
1 teaspoon ground cinnamon
1/2 teaspoon ground nutmeg
1/2 cup firmly packed brown sugar
**2 large pears, peeled, cored and
    finely chopped**
**3/4 cup chopped toasted pecans
    (see Chef's tip)**
2 eggs
1 1/2 cups milk
1 teaspoon vanilla extract
1/2 cup unsalted butter, melted

6 pecan halves, to decorate
confectioners' sugar, to dust

1 Preheat the oven to 425°F. Brush a 6-cup jumbo muffin pan with melted butter or oil. Sift the flours, cinnamon and nutmeg into a large mixing bowl, and stir in the sugar, pears and pecans.

2 Whisk the eggs, milk and vanilla together and pour them into the well in the dry ingredients. Add the butter and stir with a metal spoon until the mixture is just combined. Do not overmix—the mixture should be lumpy.

3 Spoon the mixture into the muffin pan, filling each cup about three-quarters full. Press a pecan onto the top of each muffin and bake for 30 minutes, or until a skewer comes out clean when inserted into the center of a muffin. Cool in the pan for 5 minutes before lifting out onto a wire rack. Dust with sifted confectioners' sugar before serving. These muffins are delicious sliced in half and served with butter.

Chef's tip To toast the nuts, spread them on a baking sheet and bake in a 350°F oven for 5–7 minutes, or until lightly browned.

Apricot muffins

These fruity muffins, made with dried apricots and whole wheat flour, are best eaten on the day they are made. You can use other fruits such as dried peaches or figs, or pumpkin pie spice in place of the cinnamon.

*Preparation time **25 minutes***
*Total cooking time **25 minutes***
Makes 12 standard muffins

1 cup chopped dried apricots
1/2 cup orange juice
1 1/2 cups all-purpose flour
1 1/3 cups whole wheat flour
1 1/2 teaspoons baking powder
1 1/2 teaspoons ground cinnamon
3/4 cup firmly packed brown sugar
3/4 cup milk
1 egg
3/4 cup unsalted butter,
   melted
confectioners' sugar,
   to dust

1 Preheat the oven to 425°F. Brush a 12-cup standard muffin pan with melted butter or oil. Place the apricots in a small bowl. Warm the orange juice and pour it over the apricots, then allow to cool.

2 Sift the flours, baking powder and cinnamon into a large mixing bowl, and return the husks to the bowl. Stir in the sugar, and make a well in the center.

3 Whisk the milk and egg together and pour into the well in the dry ingredients with the butter, apricots and juice. Stir with a metal spoon until the mixture is just combined. Do not overmix—the mixture should be lumpy.

4 Spoon the mixture into the muffin pan, filling each cup about three-quarters full. Bake for 20 minutes, or until a skewer comes out clean when inserted into the center of a muffin. Cool in the pan for 5 minutes before lifting out onto a wire rack. Sprinkle the tops of the muffins lightly with sifted confectioners' sugar.

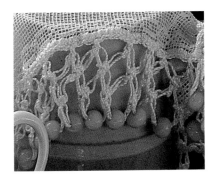

Mocha muffins

Mocha was originally the name of a strong Arabian coffee with a distinctive aroma, shipped from Yemen's port of Mocha. Today, mocha often refers to a hot chocolate- and coffee-flavored drink or to the combination of these two flavors used in cakes, cookies or, as in this case, muffins.

*Preparation time **20 minutes***
*Total cooking time **25 minutes***
Makes 12 standard muffins

1¹/₂ cups milk
4 teaspoons instant coffee powder or granules
1²/₃ cups self-rising flour
1²/₃ cups all-purpose flour
¹/₃ cup unsweetened cocoa
¹/₂ cup firmly packed brown sugar
2 eggs, lightly beaten
³/₄ cup unsalted butter, melted
¹/₂ cup whipping cream, whipped
cocoa mix, to dust

1 Preheat the oven to 425°F. Brush a 12-cup standard muffin pan with melted butter or oil. Heat the milk in a small saucepan over medium heat, without boiling, and add the coffee powder or granules. Stir until dissolved, then set aside to cool.

2 Sift the flours and cocoa into a large mixing bowl, stir in the sugar and make a well in the center. Add the milk mixture, the eggs and the butter to the well in the dry ingredients, and stir with a metal spoon until just combined. Do not overmix—the mixture should be lumpy.

3 Spoon the mixture into the muffin pan, filling each cup about three-quarters full. Bake for 20 minutes, or until a skewer comes out clean when inserted into the center of a muffin. Cool the muffins in the pan for 5 minutes before lifting out onto a wire rack to cool completely before decorating.

4 Top each of the muffins with a generous spoonful of whipped cream, and then dust lightly with the sifted cocoa mix.

Chocolate and walnut muffins

These rich dark chocolate muffins freeze very well—simply allow to cool completely and seal in airtight freezer containers or bags for up to a month. To serve, thaw the muffins at room temperature and reheat in a 350°F oven if desired.

*Preparation time **20 minutes***
*Total cooking time **20 minutes***
Makes 12 standard muffins

2 cups self-rising flour
¹/₂ cup all-purpose flour
¹/₂ teaspoon baking powder
¹/₄ cup unsweetened cocoa
²/₃ cup unsalted butter
³/₄ cup firmly packed
   brown sugar
³/₄ cup milk
2 eggs
³/₄ cup chopped walnuts
I cup coarsely chopped
   semisweet chocolate
confectioners' sugar, to dust

1 Preheat the oven to 400°F. Grease a 12-cup standard muffin pan with melted butter or oil. Sift the flours, baking powder and cocoa into a mixing bowl.

2 Stir the butter and sugar in a small saucepan over low heat until the butter is melted and the sugar has dissolved. Remove from the heat. Whisk the milk and eggs together.

3 Add the chopped walnuts and chocolate to the dry ingredients, and make a well in the center. Pour the butter and egg mixtures into the well, and stir with a metal spoon until the mixture is just combined. Do not overmix—the mixture should be lumpy.

4 Spoon into the muffin pan, filling each cup about three-quarters full. Bake for 15–18 minutes, or until a skewer comes out clean when inserted into the center of a muffin. Cool in the pan for 5 minutes before lifting out onto a wire rack. Dust with the sifted confectioners' sugar.

Orange and poppy seed muffins

*Countless poppy seeds are scattered liberally throughout these mufffins, filling them with
a delightful flavor and delicate crunch.*

Preparation time **20 minutes**
Total cooking time **20 minutes**
Makes 10 standard muffins

2¹/2 cups self-rising flour
¹/4 teaspoon baking powder
¹/4 cup sugar
2¹/2 tablespoons poppy seeds
2 tablespoons finely grated orange rind
¹/3 cup unsalted butter
¹/3 cup apricot jam
2 eggs
¹/3 cup buttermilk
confectioners' sugar, to dust

1 Preheat the oven to 400°F. Grease 10 cups of a
12-cup standard muffin pan with a little melted butter
or oil and fill the remaining 2 cups with water. Sift the
flour, baking powder and sugar into a large bowl. Stir in
the poppy seeds and grated orange rind, and make a well
in the center.

2 Melt the butter and jam in a small saucepan over low
heat, stirring until smooth. Remove from the heat.
Whisk the eggs and buttermilk together. Add the butter
and egg mixtures to the well in the dry ingredients. Stir
with a metal spoon until the mixture is just combined.
Do not overmix—the mixture should be lumpy.

3 Spoon the mixture into ten cups of the muffin pan,
filling each cup about three-quarters full. Bake for
12–15 minutes, or until a skewer comes out clean when
inserted into the center of a muffin. Cool the muffins in
the pan for 5 minutes before lifting out onto a wire rack.
Dust with sifted confectioners' sugar before serving.
These orange and poppy seed muffins are delicious
served with butter.

Prune muffins

The combination of rich dark prunes and rolled oats makes this an excellent muffin for the health conscious. The crunchy sweet oat topping is optional, but is highly recommended for its added flavor and crunch.

Preparation time 25 minutes
Total cooking time 20 minutes
Makes 12 standard muffins

1 1/4 cups self-rising flour
2/3 cup all-purpose flour
1/2 cup whole wheat flour
3/4 cup teaspoon baking powder
1/2 cup firmly packed brown sugar
1/2 cup rolled oats
1/2 cup chopped pitted prunes
2 eggs
1 cup milk
1/3 cup unsalted butter, melted

STREUSEL TOPPING
4 teaspoons all-purpose flour
1/2 teaspoon ground cinnamon
1/4 teaspoon ground nutmeg
1/4 cup firmly packed brown sugar
1/3 cup rolled oats
1 tablespoon unsalted butter, melted

1 Preheat the oven to 425°F. Brush a 12-cup standard muffin pan with melted butter or oil. Sift the flours and baking powder into a large mixing bowl, returning the husks to the bowl. Stir in the sugar, oats and prunes, and make a well in the center.

2 Whisk together the eggs and milk and pour into the well in the dry ingredients along with the butter. Stir with a metal spoon until just combined. Do not overmix—the mixture should be lumpy. Spoon the mixture into the muffin pan, filling each cup about three-quarters full.

3 To make the streusel topping, place all the ingredients in a small bowl and mix well. Sprinkle the topping over the tops of the unbaked muffins, and press gently. Bake for 20 minutes, or until a skewer comes out clean when inserted into the center of a muffin. Cool the muffins in the pan for 5 minutes before lifting out onto a wire rack.

Chocolate-chip muffins

If chocolate chips are not available to make these decadent chocolate-chip muffins, you can simply use chopped semisweet chocolate.

Preparation time **15 minutes**
Total cooking time **30 minutes**
Makes 6 jumbo muffins

1³/4 **cups self-rising flour**
2/3 **cup all-purpose flour**
1/3 **cup unsweetened cocoa**
1/2 **cup firmly packed brown sugar**
1¹/2 **cups semisweet chocolate chips**
2 **eggs**
1¹/2 **cups buttermilk**
1/3 **cup unsalted butter, melted**
3 **tablespoons semisweet chocolate chips, extra**
confectioners' sugar, to dust

1 Preheat the oven to 425°F. Brush a 6-cup jumbo muffin pan with melted butter or oil. Sift the flours and cocoa powder into a large mixing bowl, stir in the sugar and chocolate chips, and make a well in the center.

2 Whisk the eggs and buttermilk together and pour into the well in the dry ingredients along with the butter. Stir with a metal spoon until just combined. Do not overmix—the mixture should be lumpy.

3 Spoon the mixture into the muffin pan, filling each cup about three-quarters full. Sprinkle with the extra chocolate chips, pressing them on gently. Bake for 30 minutes, or until a skewer comes out clean when inserted into the center of a muffin. Cool the muffins in the pan for 5 minutes before lifting out onto a wire rack. Dust with the sifted confectioners' sugar before serving.

Bran muffins

High in fiber and sweetened only with honey, these healthy muffins make an excellent start to the day. They are best eaten warm with a little butter on the day they are made.

*Preparation time **20 minutes***
*Total cooking time **25 minutes***
Makes 12 standard muffins

1³/4 cups self-rising flour
I cup unprocessed bran
I ¹/3 cups golden raisins
¹/3 cup unsalted butter
¹/3 cup honey
2 eggs
I cup plain yogurt

1 Preheat the oven to 425°F. Line a 12-cup standard muffin pan with paper bake cups. Sift the flour into a large mixing bowl, stir in the bran and raisins, and make a well in the center.

2 Place the butter and honey in a small saucepan, and stir over low heat until melted and well mixed. Remove from the heat. Whisk together the eggs and yogurt, and pour into the well in the dry ingredients along with the butter and honey mixture. Stir with a metal spoon until just combined. Do not overmix—the mixture should be lumpy.

3 Spoon the mixture into the muffin pan, filling each cup about three-quarters full. Bake for 20 minutes, or until a skewer comes out clean when inserted into the center of a muffin. Cool the muffins in the pan for 5 minutes before lifting out onto a wire rack. Serve warm or cold with butter.

Chef's tip Paper bake cups are available from most supermarkets. If they are not available, brush the muffin pan with melted butter or oil before using.

Fruit and nut muffins

*This recipe calls for mixed dried fruit, pecans and hazelnuts; however, one could use any
single type of dried fruit with either walnuts or almonds, or a combination of nuts.*

Preparation time **20 minutes**
Total cooking time **20 minutes**
Makes 12 standard muffins

1³/4 cups self-rising flour
¹/3 cup whole wheat flour
¹/2 teaspoon baking powder
1¹/2 teaspoons ground cinnamon
¹/2 teaspoon ground nutmeg
¹/2 teaspoon ground allspice
1 teaspoon ground ginger
2/3 cup unsalted butter
¹/4 cup firmly packed brown sugar
¹/4 cup light molasses
3/4 cup milk
2 eggs
1 cup mixed dried fruit, such as golden and seeded
     raisins, currants, chopped citron, apricots and glacé
     (candied) cherries (see Chef's tip)
2/3 cup chopped pecans
¹/3 cup chopped hazelnuts
confectioners' sugar, to dust

1 Preheat the oven to 400°F. Grease a 12-cup standard
muffin pan with melted butter or oil. Sift the flours,
baking powder, cinnamon, nutmeg, allspice and ginger
into a large mixing bowl. Return the husks to the bowl.
2 Stir the butter, sugar and molasses in a small
saucepan over low heat until the butter melts and the
sugar dissolves. Remove from the heat. Whisk the milk
and eggs together.
3 Stir the dried fruits, pecans and hazelnuts into the
dry ingredients, and make a well in the center. Pour the
butter and egg mixtures into the well and stir with a
metal spoon until just combined. Do not overmix—the
mixture should be lumpy.
4 Spoon the mixture into the muffin pan, filling each
cup about three-quarters full. Bake for 15–18 minutes,
or until a skewer comes out clean when inserted into
the center of a muffin. Cool the muffins in the pan for
5 minutes before lifting out onto a wire rack. Dust with
sifted confectioners' sugar before serving. These muffins
are delicious served with butter.

Chef's tip You can of course create your own
combination of mixed dried fruit to suit your taste.

Chocolate and orange muffins

A classic combination of flavors, these rich muffins have a dark creamy topping made with chocolate and Cointreau, the sweet orange-flavored liqueur.

*Preparation time **25 minutes***
*Total cooking time **25 minutes***
Makes 12 standard muffins

I cup chopped semisweet chocolate
1/3 cup unsalted butter, chopped
2 1/2 cups self-rising flour
2/3 cup all-purpose flour
1/4 cup unsweetened cocoa
1/4 cup sugar
2 eggs
I cup milk
I tablespoon finely grated orange rind

TOPPING
1 1/3 cups chopped semisweet chocolate
1/4 cup unsalted butter, chopped
I tablespoon Cointreau

shreds of orange rind, to decorate

1 Preheat the oven to 425°F. Brush a 12-cup standard muffin pan with melted butter or oil. Place the chocolate and butter in the top of a double boiler over barely simmering water. Stir occasionally, until the chocolate and butter are melted. Remove from the heat.

2 Sift the flours and cocoa powder into a large mixing bowl. Stir in the sugar and make a well in the center. Whisk the eggs, milk and orange rind together, and pour into the well in the dry ingredients along with the melted chocolate mixture. Stir with a metal spoon until just combined. Do not overmix—the mixture should be lumpy.

3 Spoon the mixture into the muffin pan, filling each cup to about three-quarters full. Bake for 20 minutes, or until a skewer comes out clean when inserted into the center of a muffin. Cool the muffins in the pan for 5 minutes, then lift out onto a wire rack to cool completely before spreading with the topping.

4 To make the topping, place the chocolate and butter in the top of a double boiler over barely simmering water. Stir occasionally, until the chocolate and butter are melted and have combined. Remove from the heat, stir in the Cointreau, and allow to cool until the topping is thick enough to spread easily on top of the muffins. Decorate the topping with the shreds of orange rind before serving.

Date and walnut muffins

These muffins are particularly suitable for lunch boxes, and can also be made as larger muffins. To do this, use a six-cup muffin pan and increase the baking time by approximately ten minutes.

Preparation time 20 minutes
Total cooking time 25 minutes
Makes 12 standard muffins

1¼ cups chopped pitted dates
⅓ cup unsalted butter
½ cup firmly packed brown sugar
1¾ cups self-rising flour
⅔ cup all-purpose flour
1 cup chopped toasted walnuts
  (see Chef's tip)
2 eggs, lightly beaten
confectioners' sugar, to dust

1 Preheat the oven to 425°F. Brush a 12-cup standard muffin pan with melted butter or oil. Place 1 cup water in a saucepan with the dates, butter and sugar, and stir over low heat until the butter has melted. Bring to a boil, then remove from the heat and allow the mixture to cool to room temperature.

2 Sift the flours into a large mixing bowl, and stir in the walnuts. Make a well in the center and pour in the date mixture along with the eggs, and stir with a metal spoon until the mixture is just combined. Do not overmix— the mixture should be lumpy.

3 Spoon the mixture into the muffin pan, filling each cup about three-quarters full. Bake for 20 minutes, or until a skewer comes out clean when inserted into the center of a muffin. Cool the muffins in the pan for 5 minutes before lifting out onto a wire rack. Dust with sifted confectioners' sugar before serving.

Chef's tip To toast the nuts, spread them on a baking sheet and bake in a 350°F oven for 5–7 minutes, or until lightly browned.

Granola muffins

There are a number of ways of eating granola—with fruit, yogurt, milk or, as in this case, as part of a muffin. These muffins are ideal served at breakfast, and are also good served with a warm fruit compote.

Preparation time **15 minutes**
Total cooking time **20 minutes**
Makes 12 standard muffins

1 1/4 **cups self-rising flour**

1/2 **cup whole wheat flour**

3/4 **teaspoon baking powder**

3/4 **cup toasted granola**

1/2 **cup firmly packed brown sugar**

2/3 **cup raisins**

1 **cup milk**

2 **eggs**

1/3 **cup unsalted butter,**
  melted

1/2 **cup toasted granola, extra**

1 Preheat the oven to 415°F. Brush a 12-hole standard muffin pan with melted butter or oil. Sift the flours and baking powder together and return the husks to the bowl. Stir in the granola, sugar and raisins, and make a well in the center.

2 Whisk the milk and eggs together, and add to the well in the dry ingredients along with the butter. Stir with a metal spoon until just combined. Do not overmix—the mixture should be lumpy.

3 Spoon the mixture into the muffin pan, filling each cup about three-quarters full. Sprinkle the extra granola on top of the unbaked muffins and press on gently. Bake for 20 minutes, or until a skewer comes out clean when inserted into the center of a muffin. Cool the muffins in the pan for 5 minutes before lifting out onto a wire rack. These muffins are delicious served warm with butter.

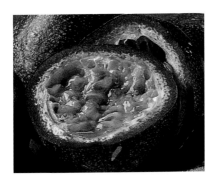

Passionfruit and yogurt muffins

The sweet tang and crunch of the passionfruit seeds, and the melt-in-the-mouth frosting,
will make these muffins appeal to all ages.

Preparation time **30 minutes**
Total cooking time **30 minutes**
Makes **12 standard muffins**

2¹/₂ cups self-rising flour
2/3 cup all-purpose flour
1/3 cup sugar
1/2 cup unsalted butter
1/4 cup honey
2 eggs, lightly beaten
I cup plain yogurt
1/2 cup passionfruit pulp (see Chef's tip)

PASSIONFRUIT FROSTING
1/3 cup unsalted butter, softened
I cup confectioners' sugar
2–3 tablespoons passionfruit pulp
  (see Chef's tip)

1 Preheat the oven to 425°F. Brush a 12-cup standard muffin pan with melted butter or oil. Sift the flours into a large mixing bowl, stir in the sugar and make a well in the center.

2 Place the butter and honey in a small saucepan, and stir over low heat until melted and blended. Remove from the heat, cool slightly, then pour into the well in the dry ingredients along with the eggs, yogurt and passionfruit pulp. Stir with a metal spoon until the mixture is just combined. Do not overmix—the mixture should be lumpy.

3 Spoon the mixture into the muffin pan, filling each cup about three-quarters full. Bake for 20–25 minutes, or until a skewer comes out clean when inserted into the center of a muffin. Cool the muffins in the pan for 5 minutes, then lift out onto a wire rack to cool completely before spreading with the frosting.

4 To make the passionfruit frosting, beat the butter and confectioners' sugar with an electric mixer until light and creamy. Beat in the passionfruit pulp until well mixed, then spread onto the muffins.

Chef's tip You will need about six large passionfruit for this recipe.

Raspberry streusel muffins

The much-loved streusel topping is used in this recipe for raspberry streusel muffins. Any type of berry could be substituted for raspberries to give perfect results every time.

*Preparation time **25 minutes***
*Total cooking time **20 minutes***
Makes 12 standard muffins

1³/4 cups self-rising flour
1¹/2 cups all-purpose flour
¹/2 cup firmly packed brown sugar
1¹/4 cups fresh or frozen raspberries
  (see Chef's tips)
2 eggs
1 cup milk
¹/2 cup unsalted butter, melted

STREUSEL TOPPING
¹/2 cup all-purpose flour
2 tablespoons unsalted butter, chilled and cubed
3 tablespoons firmly packed brown sugar

1 Preheat the oven to 425°F. Brush a 12-cup standard muffin pan with melted butter or oil. Sift the self-rising and all-purpose flour into a large mixing bowl, stir in the brown sugar and raspberries, and make a well in the center.

2 Whisk the eggs and milk together, and pour into the well in the dry ingredients along with the butter. Stir with a metal spoon until just combined. Do not overmix—the mixture should be lumpy. Spoon the mixture into the muffin pan, filling each cup about three-quarters full.

3 To make the topping, place the flour, butter and sugar in a small bowl, and rub together with your fingertips until crumbly. Sprinkle on top of the unbaked muffins, and press on gently.

4 Bake for 20 minutes, or until a skewer comes out clean when inserted into the center of a muffin. Cool the muffins in the pan for 5 minutes before lifting out onto a wire rack.

Chef's tips Different types of berries, such as blackberries, boysenberries or loganberries, can be used instead of the raspberries. Large berries, such as strawberries, should be chopped into smaller pieces.

If you are using frozen raspberries, use them straight from the freezer. Do not allow them to thaw, or they will discolor the muffin mixture.

Streusel—the German for "sprinkle"—is a crumbly topping comprising flour, sugar and butter.

Pumpkin muffins

The delicate flavor of spices, and the mild, sweet flesh of the pumpkin are a perfect combination.
These muffins are ideal for picnics, breakfast or mid-morning snacks.

Preparation time **15 minutes**
Total cooking time **40 minutes**
Makes 12 standard muffins

I lb. peeled and cubed pumpkin (see Chef's tip)
1²/3 cups self-rising flour
²/3 cup whole wheat flour
²/3 cup all-purpose flour
I teaspoon baking powder
¹/2 teaspoon ground cinnamon
¹/4 teaspoon ground nutmeg
¹/2 cup firmly packed brown sugar
2 eggs
¹/2 cup vegetable oil
¹/2 cup milk
I teaspoon vanilla extract

1 Preheat the oven to 425°F. Brush a 12-cup standard muffin pan with melted butter or oil. Steam or microwave the pumpkin until tender, then drain well and mash to measure 1 cup. Allow to cool.

2 Sift the flours, baking powder, cinnamon and nutmeg into a large mixing bowl, returning the husks to the bowl. Stir in the brown sugar and make a well in the center.

3 Whisk the eggs, oil, milk and vanilla together, and pour into the well in the dry ingredients with the pumpkin. Stir with a metal spoon until just combined. Do not overmix—the mixture should be lumpy.

4 Spoon the mixture into the muffin pan, filling each cup about three-quarters full. Bake for 20–25 minutes, or until a skewer comes out clean when inserted into the center of a muffin. Cool the muffins in the pan for 5 minutes before lifting out onto a wire rack.

Chef's tip If you want, you can substitute 1 cup canned puréed pumpkin for the fresh pumpkin.

Pumpkin muffins are a perfect accompaniment to soup for a light lunch served with a crisp green salad.

Corn muffins

Cornmeal is used here with sweet corn kernels to produce these bright savory muffins. They are superb served warm with butter and honey.

*Preparation time **15 minutes***
*Total cooking time **20 minutes***
*Makes **12 standard muffins***

1³/4 cups self-rising flour
pinch of cayenne pepper
I cup yellow cornmeal
¹/2 cup finely shredded Cheddar
I ¹/4 cups drained canned corn kernels
  (see Chef's tip)
I cup milk
2 eggs
¹/3 cup unsalted butter, melted

1 Preheat the oven to 425°F. Brush a 12-cup standard muffin pan with melted butter or oil. Sift the flour and cayenne pepper into a large bowl. Stir in the cornmeal, cheese and corn kernels, and make a well in the center.

2 Whisk the milk and eggs together, and pour into the well in the dry ingredients along with the butter. Stir with a metal spoon until just combined. Do not overmix—the mixture should be lumpy. Spoon the mixture into the muffin pan, filling each cup about three-quarters full.

3 Bake for 20 minutes, or until a skewer comes out clean when inserted into the center of a muffin. Cool the muffins in the pan for 5 minutes before lifting out onto a wire rack.

Chef's tips You can also use fresh or frozen corn kernels. Cook them in boiling water until they are tender, then drain and cool before using.

Corn muffins are a perfect accompaniment to soup.

Seeded cheese muffins

These savory muffins are so simple to prepare, and make a delicious change from French or Italian bread for a deli lunch. Alternatively, serve with cheese and pickles for a quick snack.

Preparation time **20 minutes**
Total cooking time **25 minutes**
Makes 12 standard muffins

1/3 cup sesame seeds
1/3 cup shelled sunflower seeds
1/3 cup pumpkin seeds (pepitas)
2 1/2 cups self-rising flour
2/3 cup all-purpose flour
pinch of salt
1/2 cup shredded Cheddar
1/2 cup grated Parmesan
2 eggs
I cup milk
1/2 cup unsalted butter, melted
I tablespoon sesame seeds, extra

1 Preheat the oven to 425°F. Brush a 12-cup standard muffin pan with melted butter or oil. Place the sesame, sunflower and pumpkin seeds (pepitas) in a skillet, and dry-fry over low heat for a few minutes, or until the sesame seeds are golden. Transfer to a large mixing bowl to cool. Sift the flours and salt onto the seeds, stir in the cheeses, and make a well in the center.
2 Whisk the eggs and milk together and add to the well in the dry ingredients along with the butter. Stir with a metal spoon until just combined. Do not overmix—the mixture should be lumpy. Spoon into the muffin pan, filling each cup about three-quarters full. Sprinkle with the extra sesame seeds.
3 Bake for 20 minutes, or until a skewer comes out clean when inserted into the center of a muffin. Cool the muffins in the pan for 5 minutes before lifting out onto a wire rack.

Cheese and herb muffins

Cheese and herb muffins are an excellent accompaniment to soups and stews.
They are also delicious spread with butter.

Preparation time **25 minutes**
Total cooking time **20 minutes**
Makes 12 standard muffins

1³/4 **cups self-rising flour**
1 **cup whole wheat flour**
1¹/2 **teaspoons baking powder**
pinch of cayenne pepper
pinch of salt
2 **tablespoons finely chopped fresh parsley**
2 **tablespoons finely chopped fresh chives**
2 **tablespoons fresh thyme leaves**
1 **cup shredded Cheddar**
2 **eggs**
1 **cup milk**
¹/2 **cup unsalted butter, melted**

1 Preheat the oven to 425°F. Brush a 12-cup standard muffin pan with melted butter or oil. Sift the flours, baking powder, cayenne pepper and salt into a large bowl, and return the husks to the bowl. Stir in the herbs and cheese, and make a well in the center.

2 Whisk the eggs and milk together and pour into the well in the dry ingredients along with the butter. Stir with a metal spoon until just combined. Do not overmix—the mixture should be lumpy.

3 Spoon the mixture into the muffin pan, filling each cup about three-quarters full. Bake for 20 minutes, or until a skewer comes out clean when inserted into the center of a muffin. Cool the muffins in the pan for 5 minutes before lifting out onto a wire rack.

Chef's tip Serve spread with butter while the muffins are still warm.

Bacon muffins

Bacon muffins are perfect for a leisurely weekend brunch with scrambled or poached eggs, or simply with butter. When making these muffins, it is very important not to overmix the batter or the muffins will be tough and rubbery.

Preparation time **25 minutes**
Total cooking time **30 minutes**
Makes 12 standard muffins

2 teaspoons oil
6 slices bacon, finely chopped
I large onion, finely chopped
2¹/2 cups self-rising flour
²/3 cup all-purpose flour
pinch of salt
I tablespoon chopped
  fresh parsley
2 eggs
I cup milk
¹/2 cup unsalted butter,
  melted

1 Preheat the oven to 425°F. Brush a 12-cup standard muffin pan with melted butter or oil. Heat the oil in a skillet and cook the bacon until it is brown and crisp. Remove from the pan and drain on crumpled paper towels. Cook the onion in the same pan until it is very soft and light golden, then allow to cool.

2 Sift the flours and salt into a large bowl, stir in the parsley, and make a well in the center. Whisk the eggs and milk together, and pour into the well in the dry ingredients. Add the melted butter, cooled bacon and onion, and stir with a metal spoon until just combined. Do not overmix—the mixture should be lumpy.

3 Spoon the mixture into the muffin pan, filling each cup to about three-quarters full. Bake for 20 minutes, or until a skewer comes out clean when inserted into the center of a muffin. Cool the muffins in the pan for 5 minutes before lifting out onto a wire rack.

Olive, rosemary and Parmesan muffins

The delicious combination of complementary flavors in these muffins makes them the ideal accompaniment to a crisp green salad on a hot summer's day.

Preparation time **25 minutes**
Total cooking time **20 minutes**
Makes 12 standard muffins

2¹/2 cups self-rising flour
²/3 cup all-purpose flour
pinch of salt
1¹/4 cups pitted and chopped black olives
¹/3 cup finely grated Parmesan
1 tablespoon finely chopped fresh rosemary
2 eggs
1 cup milk
¹/2 cup unsalted butter, melted

1 Preheat the oven to 425°F. Brush a 12-cup standard muffin pan with melted butter or oil. Sift the flours and salt into a large bowl, stir in the olives, Parmesan and rosemary, and make a well in the center.

2 Whisk the eggs and milk together and pour into the well in the dry ingredients along with the butter. Stir with a metal spoon until just combined. Do not overmix—the mixture should be lumpy. Spoon the mixture into the muffin pan, filling each cup about three-quarters full.

3 Bake for 20 minutes, or until a skewer comes out clean when inserted into the center of a muffin. Cool the muffins in the pan for 5 minutes before lifting out onto a wire rack.

Red pepper and feta muffins

*These muffins are best eaten on the day they are made. If this is impractical, however,
simply reheat in a 350°F oven for a few minutes before serving.*

Preparation time 30 minutes
Total cooking time 30 minutes
Makes 12 standard muffins

I large red bell pepper
2¹/₂ cups self-rising flour
²/₃ cup all-purpose flour
pinch of salt
I cup crumbled feta cheese
2 eggs
I cup milk
¹/₂ cup unsalted butter, melted

1 Preheat the oven to 425°F. Brush a 12-cup standard muffin pan with melted butter or oil. Remove the seeds and membrane from the red pepper, and cut it into large flattish pieces. Place under a preheated broiler until the skin blackens and blisters, then transfer to a plastic bag to cool. Peel away and discard the skin, and chop the flesh.

2 Sift the flours and salt into a large bowl, stir in the red pepper and feta, and make a well in the center.

3 Whisk the eggs and milk together, and pour into the well in the dry ingredients along with the butter. Stir with a metal spoon until just combined. Do not overmix—the mixture should be lumpy.

4 Spoon the mixture into the muffin pan, filling each cup about three-quarters full. Bake for 20 minutes, or until a skewer comes out clean when inserted into the center of a muffin. Cool the muffins in the pan for 5 minutes before lifting out onto a wire rack.

Ham and cheese muffins

Delicious served warm with a vegetable soup or tomato salad, these muffins can also be made with smoked ham, Gruyère cheese or a tablespoon of chopped fresh herbs.

*Preparation time **20 minutes***
*Total cooking time **25 minutes***
Makes 12 standard muffins

3 scallions, finely chopped
I teaspoon oil
2¹/₂ cups self-rising flour
²/₃ cup all-purpose flour
pinch of salt
pinch of powdered mustard
I¹/₄ cups chopped ham
I cup shredded Cheddar
2 eggs
I cup milk
¹/₂ cup unsalted butter, melted

1 Preheat the oven to 425°F. Brush a 12-cup standard muffin pan with melted butter or oil. In a skillet, fry the scallions in the oil for 2–3 minutes, or until soft. Sift the flours, salt and powdered mustard into a large bowl, and season well with freshly ground black pepper. Stir in the ham, cheese and scallions, and make a well in the center.

2 Whisk the eggs and milk together and add to the well in the dry ingredients along with the butter. Stir with a metal spoon until just combined. Do not overmix—the mixture should be lumpy.

3 Spoon the mixture into the muffin pan, filling each cup about three-quarters full. Bake for 20 minutes, or until a skewer comes out clean when inserted into the center of a muffin. Cool the muffins in the pan for 5 minutes before lifting out onto a wire rack.

Chef's techniques

◆

Preparing and filling the pan

If a recipe makes 6 jumbo muffins, you can use a 12-cup pan and make 12 standard muffins.

Lightly brush each cup of the muffin pan with melted butter or oil, or spray with nonstick cooking oil.

Alternatively, place a paper bake cup in each cup of the muffin pan.

Gently spoon the muffin mixture into the prepared pan, using another spoon to scrape the mixture off.

Melt-and-mix method

This is the most common method used to prepare muffins, resulting in a light, moist texture.

Sift the flours into a large mixing bowl, stir in the sugar and remaining dry ingredients. Make a well in the center.

Melt the butter in a small saucepan, then remove from the heat and allow to cool slightly.

Combine the eggs and milk in a bowl or 4-cup measure, then pour into the well in the dry ingredients along with the cooled butter.

Using a large metal spoon, incorporate the wet and dry mixtures with a folding motion. Stir until just combined, but do not overmix—the batter should be lumpy—otherwise the muffins will be tough and rubbery.

Testing for doneness

Bake the muffins as directed in the recipe, then test if they are cooked using either of these methods.

If a skewer comes out clean when inserted into the center of a muffin, the muffins are cooked.

If a muffin springs back when lightly pressed with your fingertips, the muffins are cooked.

Removing from the pan

Most muffins should be left for 5 minutes to set before they are removed from the pan.

Gently loosen the edges of the muffins with a palette knife.

Carefully lift the muffins from the pan and place on a wire rack to cool.

Streusel topping

Streusel toppings add a lovely crunchy texture to muffins.

Sprinkle the streusel topping evenly over the top of the unbaked muffin mixture.

Freezing muffins

Muffins will freeze well for up to a month. You can wrap them individually, and enjoy one at a time.

Place the muffins in a freezer bag and remove as much air as possible. Seal well, and freeze. When ready to use, thaw at room temperature or wrap in foil and heat in a 350°F oven.

First published in the United States in 1998 by Periplus Editions (HK) Ltd., with editorial offices at
153 Milk Street, Boston, Massachusetts 02109.

Murdoch Books and Le Cordon Bleu thank the 32 masterchefs of all the Le Cordon Bleu Schools, whose knowledge and
expertise have made this book possible, especially: Chef Cliche (MOF), Chef Terrien, Chef Boucheret, Chef Duchêne (MOF),
Chef Guillut, Chef Steneck, Paris; Chef Males, Chef Walsh, Chef Hardy, London; Chef Chantefort, Chef Bertin, Chef Jambert,
Chef Honda, Tokyo; Chef Salembien, Chef Boutin, Chef Harris, Sydney; Chef Lawes, Adelaide; Chef Guiet, Chef Denis, Ottawa.
Of the many students who helped the Chefs test each recipe, a special mention to graduates David Welch and Allen Wertheim.
A very special acknowledgment to Directors Susan Eckstein, Great Britain, and Kathy Shaw, Paris, who have been responsible for
the coordination of the Le Cordon Bleu team throughout this series.

The Publisher and Le Cordon Bleu also wish to thank Carole Sweetnam for her help with this series.

First published in Australia in 1998 by Murdoch Books®

Managing Editor: Kay Halsey
Series Concept, Design and Art Direction: Juliet Cohen
Editor: Elizabeth Cotton, Justine Upex
Food Director: Jody Vassallo
Food Editors: Kathy Knudsen, Dimitra Stais, Tracy Rutherford
US Editor: Linda Venturoni Wilson
Designer: Michèle Lichtenberger
Photographer: Andre Martin
Food Stylist: Mary Harris
Food Preparation: Tracy Rutherford
Chef's Techniques Photographer: Reg Morrison
Home Economists: Michelle Lawton, Kerrie Mullins, Kerrie Ray

Library of Congress catalog card number: 98-85718
ISBN 962-593-445-6

Front cover: Blueberry muffins (shown with whipped cream and fresh blueberries)

Distributed in the United States by
Charles E. Tuttle Co., Inc.
RR1 Box 231-5
North Clarendon, VT 05759
Tel: (802) 773-8930
Fax: (802) 773-6993

Printed in Singapore

05 04 03 02 01 00 99 98 10 9 8 7 6 5 4 3 2 1

Important: Some of the recipes in this book may include raw eggs, which can cause salmonella poisoning.
Those who might be at risk from this (the elderly, pregnant women, young children and those suffering
from immune deficiency diseases) should check with their physicians before eating raw eggs.